PURCELL

Te Deum laudamus
& Jubilate Deo in D

FOR ST CECILIA'S DAY 1694

vocal score (english text)

Order No: NOV 070427

NOVELLO PUBLISHING LIMITED

Te Deum laudamus

for two sopranos, two altos, tenor & bass soli,
S(S)ATB, trumpets, strings & organ

Edited by J. F. Bridge

In this edition of Purcell's *Te Deum in D* for voices and instruments, I have endeavoured to give a faithful rendering of the Composer's intentions. Having recently acquired the original autograph of this interesting work, I have been enabled to correct between twenty and thirty mistakes made in the first printed copy (1697), many of which have been continued in every succeeding edition. The additions made by Dr. Boyce in 1755 (which made the work fully one-third longer) have been eliminated; and Purcell's harmonies, which in many places were unjustifiably changed, have been restored. The work is scored for Strings, Trumpets, and of course, Organ.

J. FREDERICK BRIDGE.

April 1895.

TE DEUM LAUDAMUS
IN D.

HENRY PURCELL,
Edited by J. F. BRIDGE, MUS. DOC.

* May be sung by all the Altos   † The passages between the brackets might be omitted, if thought desirable.

‡ May be sung by all the Tenors.

8225.

Prophets praise

(praise) . . . Thee. The no

f *p*

(no) - ble ar - my of Mar - tyrs praise Thee.

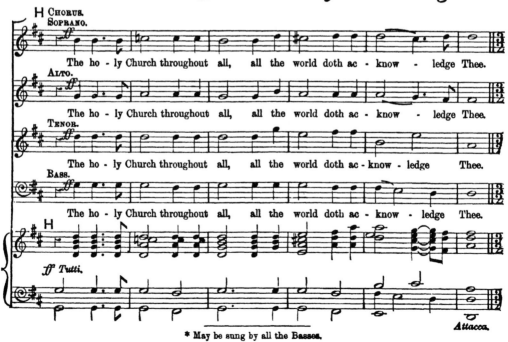

H CHORUS.
SOPRANO.

ff The ho - ly Church throughout all, all the world doth ac - know - ledge Thee.

ALTO.

ff The ho - ly Church throughout all, all the world doth ac - know - ledge Thee.

TENOR.

ff The ho - ly Church throughout all, all the world doth ac - know - ledge Thee.

BASS.

ff The ho - ly Church throughout all, all the world doth ac - know - ledge Thee.

H

ff Tutti.

Attacca.

* May be sung by all the Basses.
8226.

* This, and "Also the Holy Ghost" may be taken by Soprani, the Altos singing the 2nd Alto part only.

womb, Thou didst not ab - hor, . . not ab - hor the

- hor the Vir - gin's womb, Thou didst not ab - hor . . . . . . the

Vir - gin's womb. When Thou hadst o - ver - come the sharp -

Vir - gin's womb. When Thou hadst o - ver - come the sharp -

- - ness of death, Thou didst o - pen the King - dom of Heav'n, Thou didst o - pen the

- ness of death, Thou didst o - pen the King - dom of Heav'n, Thou didst

King - - - dom of Heav'n . . to . . all, to all . . . .

o - - - . pen the King - - . dom of Heav'n to all, . . ,

rall.

. . . . *[to all]* . . be - liev - ers.

. . . . to all . . . . . . be - liev - ers.

rall.

rall.

M
VERSE (OR SEMI-CHORUS).
Allegro. 1st SOPRANO.

mf *cres.*

Thou sit - test at the right hand, at the right hand of God, in the

VERSE (OR SEMI-CHORUS). 2nd SOPRANO.

mf

Thou sit - test at the right hand of God,

M
Allegro. ♩ = 96.

mf Org. *cres.*

* These words may be inserted, if desired.

* May be sung by a Soprano.

world with - out end, with-out . . . end. . . . . .

end, world . . . . with - out end. . . . .

end, ev - er world with-out . . end. . . . . .

. . . . *Trombe.* end. . . . . .

Slow, con espress. ALTO.*

Vouch - safe, O . . . .

Slow, con espress. ♩ = 54.

p Str. *Org.* *Str.*

cres.

Lord, to keep us this day with - out . . . . sin.

cres.

O Lord, O Lord, have mer - cy, have

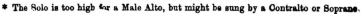

* The Solo is too high for a Male Alto, but might be sung by a Contralto or Soprano.
8226.

mer - cy,   have mer-cy up-on.. us,   have mer-cy,   mer - -

. . . . cy up - on   us.   O . . .

. . . . Lord,   O . . . . .

Lord,   let Thy mer - cy,   let Thy

mer - cy light - - - - - - - - - - - - - - - en up

- on us, as our trust . . . .

. . . . is.. in Thee, as our trust . . . .

. . . . . *[as our trust] . . . . . is.. in Thee.

* These words may be inserted, if desired.

er, nev - er, nev - er be con - found - - - ed,

- found - - - - ed, let - - - - me

me nev - er, nev - er be con - found - ed, let me nev - er, nev - er,

be con - found - ed, let me nev - er, nev - er, nev - er,

Trombe.

rall.

let me nev - er, nev - er, nev - er, nev - er be con - found - ed.

rall.

nev - er, nev - er, nev - er, nev - er, nev - er be con - found - ed.

rall.

nev - - - er, nev - er, be con - found - ed

rall.

nev - - - er, nev - er, be con found - ed.

rall.

Jubilate Deo

for treble, alto & bass soli,
S(S)ATB, trumpets, strings & organ

Edited by Watkins Shaw

This Jubilate is the companion to a setting of the Te Deum in the same key by Henry Purcell. Both compositions were first performed on St Cecilia's Day, 1694, in St Bride's Church, London. They were subsequently adopted for use on all the principal festal occasions, such as National Thanksgivings, the Festival of the Sons of the Clergy, and provincial music meetings such as those of the Three Choirs. They retained their popularity until Handel's Dettingen setting superseded them fifty years later.

Sources

(A) The first edition, published posthumously in 1697.
(B) British Museum, Harl. MS 7341, written by Thomas Tudway in 1718.
(C) York Minster MS score.
(D) Memorial Library of Music, Stanford University, California, MS score, perhaps in Purcell's holograph, formerly belonging to Sir Frederick Bridge.

There is another MS at the Royal Academy of Music, London ; but at the time when this edition was being prepared, in the aftermath of war conditions, it could not be found.

Add. MSS 9075, 17840, and 33568, in the British Museum, are later MSS of little importance, and have not been systematically collated for this edition.

The work was edited for the Purcell Society (vol. XXIII) by Alan Gray in 1923. Gray mentioned all the sources listed above, including the R.A.M. MS, but based his edition on (A) and (D). In spite of the many variants, he gave only the sketchiest collation, omitted various interesting details, and chose one reading or another without apparent system, including some not vouched for in his sources. The present text, therefore, is a new one, directly based on original sources, and differing somewhat from that of the Purcell Society. It is designed to supplement the performing edition of the Te Deum prepared by Bridge in 1895.

Editorial Practice

All indications of style and speed are editorial. In certain passages the note-values have been reduced and the barring altered ; these changes are described in footnotes.

A few *appoggiature* have been added to the vocal solo parts. These are shown as small notes, and should be given the values of the notes used. The shakes are editorial, except on page 4 (trumpet) from (D), and on pages 7 and 8 (voice parts) from (C).

Wherever the patterns ♩.. 𝅘𝅥𝅰 and ⌐· 𝅘𝅥𝅰 occur, the sources have ♩. ♪ and ⌐ ♪ respectively. The group 𝅘𝅥𝅮𝅘𝅥𝅮 in the sources has sometimes been replaced by 𝅘𝅥𝅮𝅮 ; these alterations are noted in the text.

Although this is a practical and not a critical edition, some of the more important variants (except in the string parts) have been shown as ossias or in footnotes. No note has been made of the omission of accidentals in any source or sources in unambiguous places where they are vouched for by another source; nor have alternatives in the underlaying of the words in the *Gloria* been noted.

The Organ Part

In passages marked 'organ continuo' the editor has provided a realization of the *basso continuo*, in small notes. The original scanty figuring is reproduced.

In passages marked 'organ score' the editor has arranged the composer's orchestral accompaniment. Purcell's characteristic string texture, with its wide spacing and crossing of the parts, does not transfer well to the keyboard. Nevertheless, the organ part here given to *O go your way* is an exact transcription into short score of the string parts. But when strings are combined with trumpets, as in the first and last movements, no such exact transcription would be in the least playable. Here the editor, by using three staves, has shown the trumpet parts almost literally on the top stave, and provided what is frankly an adaptation of the string parts on the two lower staves, playable, except when the trumpets are silent, by left hand and pedals alone.

The following are suggestions for registration:
TRUMPET PARTS : *not* a tuba or heavy-pressure stop, but one of light, clear, telling tone.
PEDAL PARTS : Clear 16-ft coupled to Choir for the 'organ continuo' passages (small type); coupled to Great for the 'organ score' passages (normal type).
ORGAN CONTINUO : Soft Choir flue-work.
ORGAN SCORE (strings) : *mf* to *f* Great flue-work.

1955   H.W. S.

Jubilate Deo in D

HENRY PURCELL
edited by WATKINS SHAW

*Time-signature originally ₃⁄₂ with notes twice the present value.

†Bar 7. Trumpet, dotted minim in sources (conventional value only). Similar points are later marked by the same sign.

2

lands,

lands, serve the Lord with glad - ness,

lands,

lands,

SOLO

Trumpet

continuo

39

with glad - ness,

O be

O be

O be

O be

3

Strings

44

joy-ful in the Lord, all, all ye lands:

joy-ful in the Lord, all, all ye lands: and come be-fore his

joy-ful in the Lord, all, all ye lands:

joy-ful in the Lord, all, all ye lands:

1) **SOLO**

continuo

49

pre - - sence with a song,

Trumpet

55

4

(ABCD)

59

1) Bar 52. *e*¹ (CD)

6

come be-fore his pre - - sence with a
come be-fore his pre - - sence with a
come be-fore his pre - sence with a
come be-fore his pre - sence, his pre - sence with a
(ABCD)
75

song.
song.
song.
song.
continuo
(ABCD)
79

6 [Expressively ♩=76]
ALTO
SOLO
Be ye sure that the Lord he, he is
Organ continuo
Man.
83

* Time-signature originally ¢ with identical note-values and barring.
18148

TREBLE *SOLO*

Be ye sure that the Lord he, he is God: it is he that hath made us

God: it is he that hath made us and —

87   6 (6   7   6) 2)

and not we our —

not we our

91

7

selves; we are his peo - ple, we are his peo - ple,

selves; we are his peo - ple, we are his peo - ple, and the

94

and the sheep of his pas - ture,

sheep of his pas - ture, we are his

97

1) Bar 87. ♯c'(D).   2) Bars 87-8. Figures in brackets from (D).   3) Bar 96. Last two notes ♯c''(C).

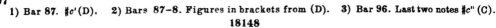

100

103

8 CHORUS
[With animation]

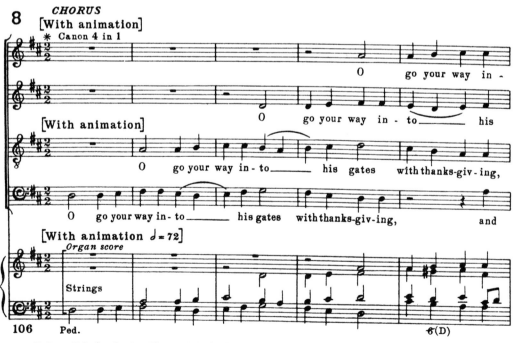

106   Ped.

1) Bar 100. ♮f' (AC).   2) Bar 101. ♮g' (ACD).   3) Bar 103. f' dotted minim (D).

*Originally notes twice the present face value, two minims to a bar—i.e. twice the number of bars as in this edition. (C) and (D) give the time-signature 2, (A) and (B) none. Add. MS. 17840, an 18th-century text, not otherwise collated here, gives the signature ₵²₁, with the first bar: o ♩ ♩ |

18148

10

1) Bar 122. No♮ (C).   2) Bar 125. Small notes from Purcell Society Edition.

*Time-signature originally ₵, with identical note-values and barring. No time-signature in (D).

18148

12

139
[149]

141
[151]

11 ***CHORUS***
[Broad, but not slow]

[Broad, but not slow]

[Broad, but not slow]

Organ score [Trumpets

[Broad, but not slow ♩=92]

Strings

153   Ped.

1) Semibreve in sources.

167

Ped.

171

1) Bar 179. This phrase for Treble 2 alone, in (D).

183

187

18

1) Bar 202. *a"*(AB); *e'''* (C)

18148